BODY AND BLOOD

Charlie Hughes is also the author of

— *Shifting for Myself* (poems)

and editor of

— *Groundwater: Contemporary Kentucky Fiction*

— *Kentucky Literary Newsletter*

Body and Blood

Poems by

Charlie Hughes

For Karen:
I hope you enjoy these
poems from the farm –

WIND PUBLICATIONS

Charlie Hughes
Thomas More, Feb 2013

International Standard Book Number 978-1-936138-15-9
Library of Congress Control Number 2010925961

First edition

Acknowledgments

Some of these poems appeared in the following magazines:

Limestone, Now & Then, The Dead Mule School of Southern Literature, Pine Mountain Sand and Gravel, Wind, and *Heartland Review.*

And in the following books:

Illumination & Praise: Poems for Elizabeth Madox Roberts and Kentucky (Des Hymnagistes Press)
Missing Mountains: We Went to the Mountaintop But It Wasn't There (Wind Publications)
Coal: A Poetry Anthology (Blair Mountain Press)
New Growth: Recent Kentucky Writing (Jesse Stuart Foundation)

for James Baker Hall

in memoriam

Contents

— Part 1 —

— Part 2 —

— Part 3 —

— Part 4 —

Part 1

What I love is near at hand,
Always, in earth and air.
— *Theodore Roethke*

Where I'm From

— after George Ella Lyon

I'm from the muddy swirl of Cecil's Creek,
the polluted currents of Salt River
where bare-assed boys swam beneath
dead hogs, flood-beached and bloated
on the limestone shelf of the river bend.
I'm from the aroma of new-mown hay,
tobacco hanging in the barn, manure
spread on the spring fields, earth freshly turned
by the John Deere plow.
I'm from Joseph's Chapel Methodist Church, sunlight
through its bare windows on Sunday morning,
the drone of Brother Ed Delaney's sermons,
those revivals on summer evenings,
all the things I never believed.
I come from Farmall tractors, New Idea mowers,
International Harvester hay balers, sweat
and chaff, straw and hay.
I'm from alfalfa and livestock,
my Jersey cow, the black lamb rejected by the ewe,
and white leghorn fryers, necks wrung on Saturday,
fried on Sunday, the milking parlor and hay loft,
pastures and the shade of maples in the yard.
I come from the Warm Morning stove, darkness
beneath piles of quilts, a gas heater
in the bathroom, ice in the bathtub.
I'm from poison ivy and Calamine lotion,
Luden's Wild Cherry cough drops, castor oil
in the Frigidaire, and my mother's hand
on my forehead.

Learning to Hit the Knuckleball, Mercer County, Kentucky, 1960

—for Don Boklage

Late summer in the shade
of the hulking tobacco barn,
listening to the drone
of fat carpenter bees,
their electric whine
drilling precisely round
tunnels into the barn's oak timbers,
I crouch in perfect stance,
Louisville Slugger shouldered,
waiting to knock
the darting black and yellow
spheres over the garden fence
and trot the base paths
to the cheering of tomatoes
and the standing adulation of corn.

Doppelgänger

What if in your 18th year you saw him
serving communion
in your grandmother's church?

What if he had your brown eyes
and hair? Your cowlick and smile?

What if after the service
strangers said to you,
Hello Harold,
and you shook their hands
and didn't say

I'm not Harold?
What if later
you asked your aunt who
that was — the one
who'd passed His body and blood?

And what if she said,
Harold Marcum —
your father used to date his mother
before the war . . .

What if this poem
is the question
you never asked your father?

Not for Naught

My first car was a ’53 Plymouth
my father bought when I was just sixteen.
Rings shot to hell, it cranked and ran okay,

but burnt more motor oil than gasoline
and belched, smelled, and smoked like Krakatoa.
I drove it like a demon through high school,

its white-wall rubber thin as onion skin,
inside the trunk a case of 30-weight,
a bald spare tire, sometimes a beer or two,

and always followed by that sulfurous fog.
It knew as well as I the road to Beth’s,
took me to my job as plumber’s stooge

and every week to town on Saturday night.
At Sam’s Pool Hall I’d shoot nine-ball ’til one
with guys who didn’t give a shit for nothing,

and all with better wheels than my old lemon.
I sold the smoker for a hundred bucks
before I left for higher education.

Elegy for a Revival

The way it was was simple in the country —
workdays dictated by the sun, dinner time
by the bell Grandmother rang, the day's end

by the plodding milk cows. The way it was
was as simple as a child of six sitting in a pew
on an August night, stirring the rancid breath

of the dead with a Mays & Sims Funeral Home fan,
head filled cocker spaniels, lightning
bugs and baseball, and the droning exhortations

of visiting preacher Brother Emory R. Jackson
this night in the Joseph's Chapel Methodist Church
having just returned from an evangelical mission

to the wilds of Borneo, wherever that was, with
his tales of saving natives for the Lord, a noble
calling, how black bodies fell to the earth in con-

vulsions before the altar, foaming at the mouth,
tongues lolling, eyeballs rolling into their foreheads.
And at last *When the Roll Is Called Up Yonder*

was sung, and the invitation for confession of faith
issued, the child remained in his seat, knowing
simply, if this was how it was, then you can have it.

Vespers

Twilight, the time
that is neither,
and the barn opens
its dark cavern to the evening.
The day has given itself
to the cool cathedral of shadows.
The barn swallows
take to their mud nests, leaving
the gray sky to the bats
darting and swooping
beneath the eaves.
The air is assaulted
by a cacophony of aromas,
alfalfa in the loft, the ferment
of silage, ammonia and muck,
steam lifting from the dark mass.
Cows lean their great weights
against one another
and rattle their hornless
heads against the feed trough.
The suck of their hooves
in the mud stirs the sour soup
of sounds, dogs howling
in the distance, the low cluck
of hens taking to roost,
the plop-plop of manure,
the burp and chew of cud,
and the soft mew of kittens
nestled in the dark recesses
beneath the manger.

They arch their tiny backs,
hiss and spit, and flash
their fishhook claws
at any intruders
in this sanctuary.

Singer

Summer afternoons when the sun
turns the lace curtains to gold
I remember the second-hand
sewing machine my father purchased
for my mother, how it ruled the dining room
from its place before the window.
I think of the long-ago late light
filtering through the curtains
to illuminate my mother
sitting in the ladder-back chair,
attention devoted to the machine,
moist drops glistening on her forehead
as she leans forward, rocking
both feet pumping the treadle,
and I hear the whirr, see the shimmer
and shimmy of the filament as it spools
to fill the silver bobbin with khaki,
the color of my father's trousers.
I remember the treasure
of pearl and gold
buttons and zippers
that overflowed its slender drawers,
the wooden spools of every size and color,
folded patterns of tulle and herringbone,
the sweet aroma of machine oil.
And I remember my father
one evening unloading the old Singer
from his Studebaker pickup,
the sweat of satisfaction on his face
as he placed it again before the window.

There, he said, presenting it to my mother,
its treadle gone, replaced by a small foot switch
to control its new electric motor.
Today, I offer tribute to my mother
for her years of toil, for her thrift,
for the eggs she traded for material and thread
at the general store, for the shirt
made from a chicken-feed sack that I still wear
in my second-grade photograph,
for my gym shorts made from boxers
on which she sewed red piping,
for every button replaced,
for every bead of sweat,
for every last stitch of breath.

Photograph of Grandmother, Golden Wells Cecil

How could you
have been the young woman
on the mantel in my parents' bedroom?
I was amazed at such beauty.
All I knew were your wrinkles,
gray hair bound in a bun
beneath your bonnet, age spots
brown on the backs of your hands,
those loose folds beneath your chin.

You stand smiling
beside French doors
where you perhaps wait, listening
for a young man on horseback,
the light caught in your diaphanous
dress, almost a halo interwoven
in your straw-colored hair, your hand
resting lightly on the door frame,
as though you are about to step
into sunlight.

I Wondered

Daddy, I wondered what was in your head.
You never told me everything you knew.
Always, you chose to leave some words unsaid.

Each night you lifted me into my bed
With rough yet gentle hands. Your words were few.
Daddy, I wondered what was in your head.

You'd been in World War II and seen the dead.
I wanted to know everything you knew,
But, always, there were words you left unsaid.

You'd pause, and place your hand on my forehead,
And teach me French, "*Come on tolly voo.*"
I knew there was much more inside your head.

There was the rifle underneath your bed,
Nearby, the .45, barrel cold and blue.
They only hinted words you left unsaid.

Each night, after you tucked me into bed
I'd question what was false and what was true.
Daddy, I wondered what was in your head.
Always, some words you chose to leave unsaid.

Elegy by a Country Graveyard

Ford tractors might do 35 or 40 on the county road.
We owners of Farmalls and Cases held
them in disdain. Put 'em under a load
Uncle Jimmy said, then see what they can do.
Maurice, a man at eighteen, tossed hay
as well as any hand. He lived next door
in a four-room tenant shack hidden
in the far corner of the cemetery,
his dad gravedigger and custodian.
When it came to work, no one could say
he shirked. Every day he earned his eight
without complaint. In midsummer,
Ed Brown paused his Ford and wagon
for Maurice, resting on the porch
before the afternoon of work resumed.
The rig hadn't ceased its roll before Maurice
hopped the hay wagon, and as the speed began
to build, walked the wagon's tongue
to ride the Ford with Ed.
Before he knew a word, he slipped.
When I arrived a crowd had gathered
where he lay, gray as lead, in the shade
of roadside oaks beside the graveyard gate.
They'd felt the wagon jolt, somebody said,
as it rolled across him.
His brother Dave knelt at his side,
mumbling softly to him
as we waited for the distant siren.
The sun was high and I squinted
at the midday sun through puffy eyes,

face stung by wasps earlier that morning.
He'd been reading a *Reader's Digest*, his mother
said, while he waited for his ride.
When the ambulance had eased away, Dave
stood there with a pack of Camels in his hand —
He gave me these — said he'd not be needing 'em.
He slipped them in the pocket of his jeans
as the siren faded in the afternoon.
Back to work, somebody said, as the crowd
began to drift toward their pickup trucks.
Goddamn Ford, Uncle Jimmy said.

The Stone

At first the boy did not hear the stone speak.
It was not a large stone.
It is only the wind in the sycamores, the boy thought,
perhaps the water babbling in the riffles of the stream.
But is the wind any more likely to speak than a stone,
or how is it that words come from water?
The stone, which had shone black as anthracite
on the stream bed, was already becoming dull in his hand.
What had called to him? What had the voice said?
He should have been paying more attention he knew.
Now the flat, heavy ovoid lay mute in the boy's palm.
What philosophy had the sun's warmth stirred
in this crystal heart he now placed in his pocket?

When I was a young girl, his mother told him,
I collected rocks. I had a shoebox full, she said,
standing by the washing machine. And taking the stone
from the pocket of his jeans, she tossed it on the shelf.
The boy carried it upstairs and laid it on his dresser.
That night before sleep a heavy roundness buried itself
in his grandmother's Mountain Stars quilt.
The stone did not speak the next day, nor the next.
Most days the boy carried the stone in his left pocket,
his Barlow in the right. Three things, his grandfather
had told him, a man ought to have on his person at all times:
a sharp pocketknife, an adequate hat, and a length of twine.
To this list the boy added the flat stone, its trusted weight
wearing threadbare the pockets of his jeans, his overalls,
his corduroys, his khakis. In time, the stone assumed

a deep luster. When he counted change from his pocket
a waitress or clerk might ask, that a good-luck charm?
Hasn't brought any yet, he'd always reply.

Walking, he knew the stone's heartbeat against his leg,
and when he sat he sensed its hard presence.
Often when alone, he'd bring the stone to light,
rub his thumb across it, heft its weight, consider its silence.
His wife wondered at the meaning of the stone,
why he carried it, who might have given it to him.
Perhaps an old girlfriend, she thought, a lost love?
The stone did not grow old. The man did.
The stone was cool in July, warm in October.
As the man grew gray the stone became lighter.
And still each day the gray man listened for the voice
he'd failed to hear that long-ago day by the stream.
One autumn afternoon his grandson found the old man sleeping
beneath a sycamore, the flat stone lying in his open palm.
It was not a large stone.
At first the boy did not hear the stone speak.

Dog Days

The whole sky is sun. Heat
rises and distorts the horizon
until the distant lies
as a shimmering lake.
These are the days of summer
when dogs lie lifeless for weeks
beneath the porch.
The jimson weed wilts
by the hog wallow
and in the skeletal limbs
of the towering sycamore
the leaves hang limp and still.
Here the wind is dead,
but far off are updrafts
where all day the black-winged
venues float in a cloudless blue.
These avian morticians wheel
and churn in circles until they boil
in some otherworld kettle.
Everything about them is mystery —
how they portend death,
how they locate their motionless prey,
how they inhale decay,
the way they are impervious
to cholera, anthrax, botulinium,
how one hunched sentinel may perch
shrouded for days on the topmost snag
of a lifeless oak.
Even now, their dark shapes gather
above our heads.

Elegy for Expectation

For a child the sun stands still as a tree.
The day is like a foot-long hotdog,
or a huge bag of Double Bubble —

enough for a lifetime. He is suspended
in time unabridged as the dictionary
and long as a dirt road mile. Christmas

arrives finally once each century,
the 4th of July, every 93 twisting miles,
Halloween as distant as Cleveland.

Then during a midlife summer rain

everything suddenly occurs on schedule.
Soon, the beard is streaked gray
as pewter, and the days

that once plodded like an ancient plow horse
now fly like Pegasus. Like Keystone Cops,
our paddy wagon careens against traffic

downhill on a one-way street, everyone
bound crazily for the same crossing. It's not
the speed we fear, but the sudden stop.

Part 2

I live and love in God's peculiar light.
— *Michelangelo*

Where I'm From, II

I'm from Salt River loam, dark and deep,
tall tobacco, barns and warehouses.
I'm from cold water and aching teeth, a rusty cup
hanging from the pump handle.
I'm from the Braxton General Store, Moon Pies
and RCs, kegs of nails, and Carter's Little Liver Pills.
I'm from summers of roast ears, white half-runners, beefsteak
tomatoes, sweat of hay loft and stench of hog pen,
polio, lockjaw, typhoid — the fear of them.
I'm from fried chicken and fried eggs, fried pork chops
and potatoes, autumns of fresh tenderloin,
lard and cracklins, lye soap and the wringer Maytag.
I'm from coal buckets, fireplace grates, and the ash pile,
the Studebaker pickup, Crescent wrench and log chain.
I'm from the freights that rattled windows in the dark of night.
I'm from Holstein and Guernsey, steam rising
from buckets of white foam.
I'm from gravel roads and road tar pooled and bubbling,
from poison ivy, honeysuckle and trumpet vine,
the wet-weather branch and the riffles of the river,
limestone palisades and fog on the dark water.
I'm from the cane pole and bobber, the trotline
and brush line, crawfish and stink-worm, snakes and toads
and cocker spaniels.
I'm from catfish and brim, croppie, turtle in the skillet.
I'm from my Western Flyer and my Dad's '47 Hudson,
and where they took me —
far enough at the time.

Young Man at Twelve Years

Unlike the old maid teachers
who ruled my grade school
in their shapeless shifts,
Miss Johnson, who taught
sixth grade
for one brief week,
attired herself in blouse and skirt.
I remember from first day the warmth
of her brown plaid,
those pleats falling just to her knees,
and her blouse, pure white, stiff
with starch, breaking over her breasts
to gather at that tiny waist.
Sitting atop her desk, science book in lap,
her auburn hair and freckles failed
to conceal the faultless
curve of cheek, or those brown eyes
that shone like the dark stars
on page twenty-three.
She wafted between the ranks of desks,
her essence the aroma of sunlight.
And at the chalkboard
her beautifully shaped long
division was applied with a perfect
jiggle of those pleats.
And the chalk dust
on those slender fingers
as they held my whole geography
text — Oh, Miss Johnson,
where did you go so soon?

Finding What I Was Born For

The night I lost it
was as hot and humid
as the shower stall echo
where that afternoon I'd sung
Danny Boy, my voice draining
down that imaginary mountainside,
stumbling over rock outcroppings
to summer in the meadows.
Lost,
though common vernacular,
is, of course, the wrong
word. I did not lose it,
nor did I trade it away.
I did not misplace it,
and it was not taken
from me. No, not
stolen. Not even
abandoned be-
side the water
where I'd parked
her sister's Chevy.
It was gladly given
to the star-filled lake,
to the brilliant stillness of night,
given wing on the dark air,
an awkward parrot untethered,
a nightingale loosed
from its cage.

Chance Encounter

Two years later
they met again.

Remember
what you said?
she asked.
It had been
something flippant,
dismissive,
words that
smoldered yet
beneath her smile.

She was blond
and wore a blue
headband,
he, a sweatshirt
and denim jeans.

It was October,
everything
red and gold.
How could they help
but fall in love?

Love Life

The black dog leaps with joy
at the sight of his mistress.
His ample tail wags his whole being.
He romps in tight circles,
upsets his water bowl.

The black dog licks her hand.
He springs to her lap,
nuzzles her crotch,
tongues her cheeks,
begs for his leash.

The black dog throbs
with an earthy pant.
His tongue lolls and drips
from an idiotic grin.
They breathe the same air.

The black dog grows weary.
He lies in the corner by the fireplace,
ear cocked for the can opener.
He thumpingly scratches his ribs,
thoughtfully licks his scrotum.

Morning Coffee

On the shortest day
of my sixty-fourth winter
I sip from the dark cup
of memory, searching
for the reason
my high-school sweetheart
chose to appear uninvited
in last night's dreams,
her dark eyes like crows
in the December sky.
I'd not seen her in forty years
and though it required twenty
to lose the ache of her,
she'd not come to mind
in more than three.
And now, without summons,
Beth steps once more
onto the stage of my consciousness,
and I again play the role
once assigned to me.
I strut and fret my hour,
graceless and awkward
as any eighteen-year-old
farm-boy senior,
once more reciting
my lines, clueless
to their meaning, but always
and again, never
deviating from that script.

Marriage Amulet

— after Nancy Willard

We are fallen and dry like pinecones.
At night we make love like porcupines,
hesitant in our touching. After many nights
we are even more prickly.

If this is aging, it is more rough
than chain-sawed pine, more sticky
than the oozing resin. Soon I will harden
into amber.

Some soul will wear my necklace near the heart.

Waiting in November

I listen for my phone but there's no ring.
I sit and watch the leaves drift through the day.
The fact that you don't call is no big thing.

Black crows roost in the oak, but they don't sing.
For hours I laze and watch the endless sway
of leafless limb and listen for your ring.

Three weeks, and yet the postman does not bring
your mail, and still no ring. I have to say
that you may never call. It's no big thing.

Your new cell phone is no tin can and string.
Your dialing finger must have turned to clay.
I listen for my phone, still there's no ring.

The crows may roost forever or take wing —
It matters not to me. Here's where I'll stay
whether or not you call. It's no big thing.

Perhaps I'll still be waiting come next spring,
or maybe not — such waiting is not play.
I listen for my phone but there's no ring.
The fact that you don't call is no big thing.

The Way of Sparrows

Ann's smile is a summer day.
When she speaks the sparrows stop their singing to listen.
Her hair is the aroma of new-mown hay, delicate
as corn silk, and the color of straw spun to gold.
Her earthy warmth tastes of the hearth
and freshly sliced lemon, and her lips
contain all that has ever been said,
her eyes blue and deep as the salt sea.

But a summer day is not always a smile.
When the clouds come, and the salt rain,
the sparrows stop their singing to weep with Ann.
Ann seeks the freedom of old age,
when, she says, she will loose her hair
to the wind, and sail by damn to the four corners.
Old Chasmo, on his peg leg, will man the helm
with his astrolabe of thumbtack and soda straw.

Spring summer winter fall the wind will waft forever
gently from the southwest — how could it not
for two in love? — and the rain be ever warm.
"Vida es dulce!" Ann will shout from the bow,
and the old lady will list to the wind and groan
in her bones at the pleasure
of unfurling her spinnaker.

Love

is black, fat, and cat-like.
In autumn she squeezes her wide
white stripe deep into the crawl
space beneath your house.
At first you hardly notice
her presence. What rises
to you is not unpleasant.
Reminiscent of something
you've encountered before,
it comes on the wind
to flirt in the shadows
of your knowing.
Gradually, it builds to an aroma
that haunts your every
sentient hour, comes to you
in the night on each breath
gulped through open mouth.
Attempts to rid yourself
of the affliction, you know
would only make it worse.
One day in summer she goes
out for a drink, you erect
a barricade behind her, lock
her out. Then sigh with relief.
That's finished, I'm over her
you say. But her off-
spring huddle in the dark
recesses beneath you.
In time, you know

something has died.
You ask yourself what have I done,
how has it come to this?
The odor of rot
permeates the house.

The Pickup

When my neighbor's wife left
her engine idling
and offered to help me dig
my car from the snowdrift —
everything went downhill from there.

Maybe it was the blush of her cheeks
against that red woolen shirt,
or the single bead of sweat
slowly growing over her left eye
in the twenty-degree morning.

Maybe it was the tan leather
of her gloves stretched tight
across her knuckles as she wielded
the shovel, or the way her jeans,
knees now wet, curved firm
over her round thighs.

It might have been the fact
she knew exactly what I needed
and where I could get it — new
links for my worn tire chains,
the Western Auto on Maple —

Maybe it was the way she lay
on her side, stretching
the tow strap to my bumper,
or maybe it was her delicate
breath condensing, that

almost inaudible grunt
as she locked the hook.

Maybe it was the warmth
that came over me inside her
Jimmy, the truck's windows clouded
by the twisting steam
lifting from the styrofoam cup
she held out to me.

Who in his right mind could refuse
such an offer? God,
you gotta love
a woman
who drives a pickup.

Love Should Grow Up

Love should grow up like
a wild iris in the fields.
— Susan Griffin

Love should grow up and quit dreaming,
face the facts. Oh, I know love is blind
in at least one eye, but it should quit making excuses,
get real, deal with its illusions and delusions of grandeur.
Love is not "a many-splendored thing."
Love can't "keep us together" or "tear us apart" or "find a way,"
it won't even "come to you" when summoned.
It should grow up and sing the truth, tell us the answer
even if we don't want to hear it.
Love is in the air, it's in the water, it's everywhere
like any rambunctious two-year-old.
In reality it's easily caught.
It's an illness, a malady, a virus, usually non-fatal,
a mixed bag of bitter pills that adults have to swallow.
While not a crime, love *is* a four-letter word,
a triple-word score on the Scrabble board of adolescence.
It's time it grew up, quit whining, being a baby, feeling
sorry for itself.
Love is an undesirable family member,
a controlling mother, a cruel temptress, the wicked step-sister,
the teen-age driver from hell,
a journey, a vicious cycle, a ride on a Harley,
a car wreck, not what it's cracked up to be,
it's got to look before crossing the street.
Love is a ball, a game, a ballgame, a contact sport
on a field of dreams, it has to quit being a push-over.
It's time for it to concentrate

on defense, ball control, managing the clock,
recognizing the blitz, be ready for the curve ball or slider,
the wild card, and quit while it's ahead.
Love is no miracle, it's a fable, a tragic story, a fairy tale,
a poem, a metaphor, a red red rose tattoo,
it's time for some hard-hitting, grown-up nonfiction.
Prince Charming has left the building
and Snow White eats that apple again each evening.
Love has to be fed, it's no king-sized bed
of roses, it's not all it needs, it has to quit
deceiving itself, feeling sorry for itself, quit pouting
quit the chick lit and chocolate and humming Indigo Girls tunes
quit doodling and drooling on its copies of *Cosmo*
quit biting its nails and wasting its money
on Dollar Store trinkets, quit chewing again
and again the bubble gum of self-deception.
Love has got to grow up and quit this foolishness
while there's still time.

October

When we are gone
there will remain
the millions of maples glittering
in their unique sameness
of crimson and gold.
The mountains, too, will remain
their tops jagged as the rocks
littering Taggert's Creek,
caves deep in their hearts,
and in the sheltered cove
the umbrella magnolia
and the faded foxglove
that blossomed
at our gaze,
the scented air we breathed,
and our shared words —
a misty dream
in the morning fog.

Brochette Dijon Flambé

She tried to marry a man already wed.
Obsessed, alone, she plotted every day
the things she'd do to get him in her bed.

Perhaps cuisine — She thought a man well fed
might quickly yield. You must admire the way
she tried to marry the man. Already wed,

he wasn't that easy. Something else instead
would be required. No end the things she'd say,
the things she'd do. To get him in her bed

she shaved her legs and dyed her hair deep red.
She spread, and though he was no easy lay,
she tried. To marry a man already wed

just wasn't in her deck of cards, he said.
And though he liked her well enough, her sway,
the things she'd do to get him in her bed,

Divorce would devastate my wife, he said,
but we can still do lunch at Chez Henré.
She tried to marry a man already wed.
The things she'd do to get him in her bed.

Women Talking

Theirs are not the voices of men.
Their words do not swagger —
they lilt like autumn warmth,
devoid of consonants.

They do not scuff their words
in the gravel. Their words
do not rattle like tools
in the pockets of Levis.

They do not whittle the oak
of their words, or lean their phrases
against the fender of a Chevy.
They do not spit, nor slouch,

nor muffle their words
in their ample denim pockets.
They do not deliver punch lines
with a fist to the shoulder.

They lay their fingers lightly
on the arm of the listener.
They do not prop the foot
of their words on the bottom rung,

nor rest the elbows of their stories
on their knees. They stand erect
high-heel weight on one leg,
and shifting to the other, cock

the ample hips of their murmurings
without missing an inflection,
or nuance of raised eyebrow.
There are no harrumphs at humor,

and never a slap on the back,
only an occasional knowing smile,
sometimes tears of merriment
or floods of sad vowels.

Part 3

There is less in this than meets the eye.

— *Tallulah Bankhead*

Where I'm From, III

I'm from brown tarpaper, four rooms
and a path at the end of Rob Road,
muddy ruts too deep
for the '47 Hudson. I'm from hogs
and hog weed, jimson weed and hemlock,
iron weed and lambs quarters, dandelion
and polk greens with fatback and boiled eggs.
I'm from the Southern Railway,
steam then diesel, windows rattling
in the 3 a.m. dark, and engineer Jimmy Cole
who nursed the whistle for the mile
to his mother's home.
I'm from the musty aroma of Salt River loam,
freshly turned and dark as the night sky.
I'm from the Big Dipper and Cassiopeia,
Orion's belt and the orange glow
of the John Deere exhaust pipe
on cool spring nights.
I'm from lofts of alfalfa and fescue,
silos of corn, the aroma of tobacco hanging
in the barn and wild onions
in the spring milk.
I'm from my mother
who stitched my shirts from feed sacks
and prepared for me
everything chocolate,
and my father who taught me
the difference between
milk bucket and slop jar.

Notes Made While Observing a Poet at the House of Great Apes and Other Primates

The house is home to many primates behind plate glass windows. One specimen (male) of a species fast approaching extinction sits beneath an obviously plastic maple. A plaque attached to the window informs us that the range of *Homo poeticus* is predominantly confined to the world's temperate climatic zones. And that scientists believe the decline of the species can possibly be traced to the free verse pandemic of the late 20th century exacerbated by that era's concurrent spate of so-called "prose" poems and the proliferation of MFA programs. Today, the solitary simian reads from a book, pausing occasionally to make awkward left-handed notations (with a red ball-point pen) in a small, spiral-bound notebook. *Poeticus* scratches his head, inspects his fingernails, then picks something from beneath the nail of his left forefinger with his teeth. Eventually, he rises and carries the notebook across his cubicle to a small table where an ancient typewriter sits beside what appears to be the remains of a TV dinner. He sits in the straight-back chair and begins to tap intermittently at the keys, pausing often to gaze at the wall, as if at some imaginary point in the distance. A young boy standing beside me raps on the window with a souvenir-shop trinket. *Poeticus* lifts his head to glance in our direction. He suddenly stands, rips the sheet from the typewriter, crushes it into a wad and flings it in our direction. Approaching the window, he stares wide-eyed at the *sapiens* standing beyond the barrier. He grunts and shows his teeth in what I imagine could be a sneer. His large blue eyes look into mine. He could be one of us.

Advertising

Gatlinburg, mid-summer,
looking up at the strolling
tourists, the kid, no more
than ten, stands before

a plate-glass window
and the taffy-pulling machine.
He's holding a hand-lettered sign

WILL WORK
FOR BEER

He grins at me
as I approach.
I say, Boy,

when your momma
gets you home
I'm gonna take
a switch to you.

How to Build a Poem

Anybody who's built a house can do it. It can have a red roof, but don't start there. Start just about anywhere else. I'd recommend the language yard. Make sure the words you choose are without knot-holes, kiln-dried and true before you lay your money on the desk. If you forget the plans check the funny papers to see what's next. Stanzas are built like rooms, each to serve a purpose. Hallways are stanza breaks. Windows will give you vision — outlook or insight as the case may be. And doorways allow entry or egress; you'll maybe want a sign that says, "This way to the Egress" for those visitors who want to hang around all night. But that's later. Construction of the poem, as with anything, is accomplished by the fitting together of components, boards or lines cut to fit, different lengths and of varying weights and angles. All the pieces are joined by verbs and glue, nails and nouns, adjectives and screws. But before we get to that there's the foundation, the central idea upon which everything rests. So we begin with a backhoe and maybe a jack-hammer—get back, jack, watch out for the bobcat. Dig out the basement and haul away the unnecessary metaphor, or save it to spread later in landscaping when you choose the proper adverbs and fertilizer for the shrubby similes you've planted. But I'm getting the cart before the horse—first there's the concrete, then you'll need some tools—saw horses and sea horses, a carpenter's square and a scribe, a musical saw and a knuckle-busting-meat-tenderizer framing hammer, a plumb bob, and several pounds of 10-penny nails—drive one any place you need a period; bend it over for a comma; forget the exclamation point—they've got no place in a poem, and for alignment of the components you'll need a micro adjuster sledge. Don't bother with a monkey wrench; there's no time for shenanigans; you're getting paid by the job. Make sure your toolbox contains a hand axe and a 12-inch flat bastard to keep it sharp. Don't forget the key-hole saw (and don't forget what you see), a hand reamer and countersink.

For the novice some sky hooks, board stretchers, and a left-handed claw hammer. For the wiring you'll need needle-nose side-cutting pliers, industrial 7-inch end nippers, an electrician's fish, and a 200-amp breaker box. A 3-cell mag will help you find dangling participles when they drop into a dark crevice. And to hold it all together you'll need to know how to nail, staple, rivet, pound and expound, screw, glue, exaggerate, and weld, braze, or solder. If you can't fit each adverb in its proper slot, relax—use a larger hammer, maybe some axle grease. And always have some silver duct tape on hand for emergencies. When you're near finished it's time for spackle and grout. Slap some mud on the rock, sand it off and paint. Stand back and take a gander. If it's not ship-shape, slip a cheater on the Sweeney wrench and torque 'er down tight. That puppy ain't going nowhere.

What I Thought at My 40th Class Reunion

—for Cathy Smith Bowers *

All I recall from my twentieth—
Alice McCoy
wore no brassiere
her low neckline

Maggie Johnson's three abortions
her cigarette
and long blond hair
that wreath of smoke

And how I spilled my plastic cup
too much to drink
knees on the floor
retrieving cubes

* Cathy Smith Bowers introduced me to this poetic form called the "minute" in her artful collection of poems *A Book of Minutes* (Iris Press).

What I Heard
at My 40th Class Reunion

Those girls sure look the worse for it,
except June Pitt's
not changed a bit.
How's she do it?

Remember Annie Ray's pimples?
Bob took her out.
Said she had 'em
on her bottom.

That awful acne lasted years.
Her husband died.
Another beer?
You're looking good.

Love Is a Barn Dance

My Uncle Bob's second wife
was an old Magnavox.
In the evenings she sat in mahogany
opulence beneath a floor lamp
in the corner of the parlor.
Each night when her tubes lit up
the old golden-eyed cyclops smelled
of burnt rubber and vomited
an out-of-tune-musical-saw static
that assaulted the ears and curled
the tongue like a copper penny.

Hank Williams lived in that radio,
in a small efficiency in the rear,
which was OK with Aunt Mildred
since she said they could use the rental income.
One night during a thunderstorm Hank died.
Dark as a well digger's bucket, the night
closed over the silent box.
If the lightning got Hank, said Uncle Bob,
probably got Jimmy Wakely, too.

Aunt Mildred was humming "hot rod Ford
and a two-dollar bill," when Uncle Bob
whispered "Whatcha got cookin?"
As the lightning flashed, Uncle Bob
hung a *Room for Rent* sign
on the volume knob, then put the kitty
on the porch, in spite of her
protestations and plea to rent —
Uncle Bob couldn't speak Catalan.

The old Magnavox closed its eye
and didn't say a word
in any damn language.
Hank and Jimmy silenced,
Aunt Mildred blew out the candle
and left it smoking on the dresser,
then she turned on Uncle Bob.

My Old Studebaker Pickup

Thing was, she was old when I got her,
the old flat-head six
always hard to start, groaning
and complaining
when I pressed the starter,
a long time to warm up,

and if I ever got anywhere with her
she made it clear
that bouncing on a bed
of gravel with those worn-out ball joints
wasn't her idea of a good time.

Never a smooth ride.

And easy to overheat,
grew hot under the slightest load,
blew off steam
like a circus calliope.

No rack and pinion,
idler arm loose,
she never steered where I told her,
and once decided on a course
toward any precipice,
the old drum brakes, squealing
and grating, played hell stopping her.

Once we went all the way
gearbox without synchronizers

to Cincinnati,
and every time I shifted
if not for double-clutch
she'd grind her teeth and kick.

That's why I traded
her in
on a sleek new model, white walls,
posi-traction rear end, Hydramatic transmission.

Every
Saturday night
you could find us at the Star-lite Drive-in.

Poem Found
on Nicholasville Road

Guaranteed
Used Tires

Buy One
Get One

The Environment — News at 11:00

Sixty-five million years ago the Cretaceous period abruptly ended when an asteroid, six miles across, traveling at a speed of nine miles per second, struck the earth, plunging twenty miles deep, exploding with the power of countless hydrogen bombs, creating a one-hundred-twenty-mile-wide crater, throwing dirt and fiery ash hundreds of miles into the atmosphere, the heat of the explosion elevating the entire earth's temperature, killing all vegetation and cloaking the earth in complete darkness for months or years, the dust in the air blocking out the sunlight thus initiating an ice age lasting hundreds of years, the result of this cataclysm being an abrupt mass extinction of most of the earth's species including the dinosaurs.

More recently, President Bush has explained, "It isn't pollution that's harming the environment. It's the impurities in our air and water that are doing it."

Turkey Vultures

They tell me that when the sun first begins to unlock the day, vultures will hunch in the mist of early morning on the topmost branch of a dead tree, cocking an eye at all creation. Then, as the earth warms and winds begin to stir, they drop from their perch, spread their wings, and allow the air to catch them. They drift and soar all the morning long on the joy of updrafts, ever climbing until they are as high as the sun, and the great river far below is a turquoise thread stitching the green wilderness. There they couple, and tumbling and cartwheeling in an ecstasy of tail-feathers, talon, and crimson pate, they plummet for what seems thousands of feet, until at the very last moment they disengage and flare out, skimming the smooth surface of the cool blue water.

Part 4

But then they danced down the street
like dingledodies, and I stumbled after
as I've been doing all my life . . .

— *Jack Kerouac*

Where I'm From, IV

I'm from Providence Road —
the house that overlooks
the cemetery — the hill that took our sleds
between the limestone slabs
and granite stones
of silent Presbyterians.
I'm from late fall and early winter,
the locust trees, those bare limbs
that rattled against the eaves at midnight,
the shadows of their knotty fingers
sifting the cold and moon-drifted snow.
I'm from the wind that leaned and shivered
against the rattling windows, and the drafts
that drove sleepers beneath the Rose
of Sharon quilt my mother pieced from scraps
of shirts, jeans, and chicken-feed sacks.
I'm from frost on the windows
and steam from the kettle
atop the Warm Morning stove,
five-gallon buckets of coal, the dust
of ash on the dining room table,
and the clash and tinkle of great suppers
of potatoes and pork chops.
I'm from the smokehouse
and the aroma of curing hams,
the washhouse and the slosh-slosh
of the wringer Maytag.
I'm from Guernseys and Jerseys
and the sweat and whine
of the hand-cranked cream separator,

the two-gallon cans, thick and heavy,
delivered to the cream station each Friday.
I'm from corn and cattle, bulls impossible
to corral, calves bawling at the fence,
nights of howling wind and dogs,
old hounds sprawling on my grandfather's porch
and the Brittany Spaniels
my mother framed
for my bedroom wall.

Bread Basket

Twelve hundred calories today —
My belly has all my attention.
This little Buddha beneath my belt
should belong to a woman. I love
my stomach if only for this single thought.
I would cup such loveliness in my palm,
slide my hand over its velvet
and into the bright ringlets below.
I would drink from its navel
the wine of sweet kisses
and taste the salt of inland seas.
It's rise and fall would be my bread and cheese
and it would know the meat of my life.
I would rest my head upon its shores
and listen to the rush of tides,
the gurgling of deep streams.
It would be my pillow
in the night, and in the morning
waken me with the rocking of gentle laughter.

Elegy for a Bird

I first noticed her in spring
fluttering at her reflection in the bay window.
A female cardinal, I thought at first glance,
gray and rust with crest. All summer I tolerated
the white droppings beneath the spattered mirrors
of Chevy and Toyota, hosed the cars twice each week,
the elusive aggravator watching, chirping peter –
peter – peter, from the yard's tallest tree.
A consultation with *Kentucky Birds* identified the culprit —
tufted titmouse, common in the wood from April.
Her call, peter – peter – peter. The book said nothing
of fascination with mirrors, or the tantalizing twin
that dwelt within. Titmouse — I'd always tittered
at that name. The plural — tit *mice*, of course.
Now my jaw was set at any utterance of it.
I tolerated her shenanigans 'til winter
when the change of seasons finally brought relief.

But then, in early April
I found the Chevy's mirrors again befouled.
I bought some .22 birdshot, then leaned
the rifle I hadn't fired in 30 years
against the wall by the French doors. I knew
I could pick her off the mirror of either vehicle
at 20 paces — and if I missed? I could always
buy a replacement mirror. I watched for days, and cat-like,
eased those French doors open half a dozen times
before she didn't fly in fright. I squeezed off a shot
that knocked her from a limb onto the driveway,
then I lifted her by the tail feathers to drop her in the fire

where I'd been burning windfall limbs.
As I turned to the house, peter – peter – peter.
Her mate descended, darting from tree to limb,
to near where she'd last rested, calling
all the while. I did what any killer
would; I chambered another round.

October Sestina

This afternoon I sit in the sun
and watch the wind whip the leaves,
a whirlwind in the autumn wood.
Light filters through the cloudy window,
through the steam lifting from my coffee.
All I know is the slow grind of calendar,

days sifting like cornmeal through a colander,
the inexorable cycle of moon and sun.
I lift the calendar from its nail, sip my coffee,
leaf through its heavy leaves.
Its pictures offer no window
to the world, or even to this wood.

It's only endless numbers. Would
I be lost without this calendar?
Would I wait each day at the window,
telling time by the creeping sun,
reading my future in tea leaves
or countless cups of French vanilla coffee?

Today it's double-chocolate flavored coffee,
but it's lost its savor. It tastes of wood,
a flavor that coats the teeth and leaves
an aftertaste to outlive this year's calendar.
The life of any mother's son
should be more than sitting by this window.

That yellow bird at the window
is not hope. This rancid cup of coffee

is no comfort. Not the heat of sun
or five cords of chain-sawed wood
split and stacked can stop the calendar
or the cold wind drifting the leaves.

When someone you love leaves
what's left is only the empty window,
meaningless digits on the calendar,
a cup of lukewarm coffee,
and this inadequate rack of firewood,
scant help for the winter sun.

But today there's sun in the leaves,
the cold stains of coffee on this calendar,
and wind in the sad wood beyond the window.

October 2000

My mother saved everything
and now we move everything,
discard this, save that, whose was this?
My father moves slowly
these days, widower three years,
but he is surely moving,
selling the ranch house to be nearer
his children.
We spend Saturday
cleansing the attic of its treasure.
Bag this, trash that, box this,
my Curt Simmons signature baseball glove,
a Captain Midnight Ovaltine decoder ring,
an old baseball my uncle caught foul
at a Cardinals game in '47, its hide
cracked and dry as my father's arms,
a quilting frame, the wood brittle
as my mother's bones when she held
it in her lap to make the quilts
my sister has already bagged,
Superman comics from the '50s,
my Hopalong Cassidy chaps and spurs,
text books warped and brown,
my *Boy Scout Handbook*, everything
we needed to know, everything
we ever thought to be.

Better to clean it out now
than after I die, my father says,
his way of offering encouragement.
We laugh at such wit.

Income tax forms and checks
from 1949 we toss in a bag
and my father shakes his head
in wonderment at why saved so long.
Fishing tackle, a broken reel with
a hickory rod Uncle Floyd fashioned
in the '30s, a bomber lure with no hooks,
they might be worth something on eBay,
every type of basket short and tall, a bucket
of coal, though none has ever burned
in this house, dolls with no stuffing,
baby buggy wheels, a brush my sister
used on her 4-H Jersey heifer, a Calumet
can containing rusty fish hooks
and lead sinkers, all plastic has decayed
in the attic heat, cracked or broken
it goes onto the pickup
to be hauled away and burned
with scrap wood and other flammables.
The grandsons hand down box
after box, then toss down the empties.
From the garage shop, one grandson
gets the table saw, the lathe
and drill press go to another.
The movers will be here Tuesday to get
the furniture, household items, concrete
statuary from the yard, everything
from the attic, everything
we ever were.

Now my father
wonders why he wanted
to move, why uproot at this stage of life,
if he wants to eat lunch at Wynette's

he'll have to drive forty miles one way.
One grandson asks him if he'll miss the house.
Nah, he answers, well, maybe a little.
It's still coming from the attic,
a tin can full of tiny tacks, we spill it,
sweep it up and discard it, plastic
Christmas tree, lights, bulbs, wreaths,
lawn decorations, more Corning Glass
bulbs, many broken and not replaced
since my father's retirement from the factory.
Did anyone find my baseball cards?
Here's a photo of my father in uniform, his
steel pot cocking his head to one side,
another photo, me from high school,
they say we look alike,
and Jesus, here are letters from my
wife to me from before
we were married, my mother
saved it all, we sort everything,
pack and discard, everything
we never were.

Blessings of Earth

Faith without works is dead.
— James 2:20

It's always been the things that I could feel
in these two hands, whatever I might heft.

I can separate the wheat from chaff,
can wield a hammer or a Crescent wrench

as well as any man, right hand or left.
I have no truck with words inferred.

The physical is much preferred.
I trust those articles produced from craft.

As for those implements cerebral —
I don't concern myself.

I know desire deferred,
too much enlightenment through self-denial.

What I know of fire will light the night.
On any day I'll choose the corporeal,

the heavy stench of hog pen,
a broken limb where rests the wren,

the carnal, or the newborn calf,
a touch of flesh to warm what lies within.

Poets bless with words,
while I prefer the laying-on of hands.

Loneliness

Before you know the real weight of loneliness
you must find yourself
in a crowd.
You must listen to the laughter of those who stand near,
and know the heavy stone in your chest.
You must pluck out that stone
and break it open — see if it contains fossils
or quartz crystal, or some bloody matrix.
You must then place a piece
in each of your pockets
where you are condemned
to carry them all of your life —
where the gravity of each piece
will weigh upon you — no one to share
the load.

Before you know the sweet sorrow of your loneliness
you must walk endless ages,
the shattered pieces throbbing
against your legs with every step —
every step no closer
to whatever goals you are destined to forget —
goals that if achieved will bring
you scant satisfaction.

Before you know loneliness
as the coldest and most exquisite black dwarf
of the universe, you must once in your life
have known a moment
of fire, of togetherness,

and then be cast into darkness —
rotten meat on the side of the highway,
the stench of yourself
calling for someone, anyone,
if only a shadow.

It is only then that you are ready for loneliness
to become your friend,
the Samaritan who binds your wounds,
gives you bread
and lifts you from the roadside
to cradle your head
against the breast of the world
and whisper to you,
I am the only one you will ever need.
I am your dark brother.

God Issues Clarification

I’ve never said that anyone should kill.
Let’s get this straight — no killing in My name!
I can't make it any clearer; it's not My will.

Tel Aviv, New York, or Louisville —
I swear, sometimes I think your minds are lame.
I’ve never said that anyone should kill.

Why do you children look for blood to spill
when all of My religions say the same
clearly stating that it’s against My will?

I am amazed and saddened at your skill
in using Me to rid yourselves of blame.
I’ve never said that anyone should kill.

You are commanded to think — don’t be a shill
for extremists who say they act in My name.
Don’t do those things that are against My will.

I thought it right that you should have free will
but you have used it to inflame and maim
and broken My commandment not to kill.
I tell you once again, IT’S NOT MY WILL.

Let Us Now Praise Famous Men

and our fathers that begat us.
— Eccl. 44:1

From dawn 'til dusk he wields the scythe and hoe.
With honest sweat and toil he earns his way.
Let us now praise the ordinary Joe.

Early to rise, today he's hay to mow.
Sun up, sun down, the light defines his day.
From dawn 'til dusk he wields the scythe and hoe.

Three grains of corn to grow, two for the crow.
He takes what comes, the skies both blue and gray.
Let us now praise the ordinary Joe.

In steaming sun he labors row on row
to till the rocky earth. It's here he'll stay
from dawn 'til dusk to wield the scythe and hoe.

When evening cool descends, the stars aglow,
a night of dream awaits his end of day.
Let slumber now the ordinary Joe.

His faith tells him his fate's not his to know.
Slow sun to moon, too soon it's clay to clay.
From dawn 'til dusk he wields the scythe and hoe.
Let us now praise the ordinary Joe.

The Dark Side of the Moon

— thanks to W.S.

The Moon approaches Earth in winter
but I would know nothing
of its inconstancies,
nothing of its wax and wane,
its perigee or apogee.
I would live alone on its dark side,
unaware of earthshine and turquoise.
I would know only the searing sun
and the dark,
diamond-studded and utterly cold.
My home would be a deep fissure
from which I'd lift my face
to the fading cosmos
and watch the planets
wander across a lonely sky.
All would be silence
save the static hiss
from the dark well of the universe.
I would be the Man in the Moon.
There would be no beginning or end
to the anything or nothing
I could or could not know.

Rio del Corazón

> *There is no memory that time will not erase,*
> *nor any pain that death will not consume.*
> — don Quixote

The river has our own deep heart.
After the weight of water muffles all words,
rests heavy as sand on the tongue,
holds all lids closed,
the only sound is the red of one's own blood.

Mañuel Tejada learned this, submerged
three days in the Rio del Corazón,
in his breast pocket a stone that would not float.
He could not get down to the dark memory
where the willows weep at every last breath,
their roots snaking through the murk
to cradle each drowned child.

Tomorrow the mariachis will sing
of winged white horses.
El Chasmo will play his trumpet
to the heavens
and from the eddies of dark foam
Mañuel will rise in a wild effervescence,
in his arms the bloated bodies
of his babies.

Only when we have forgotten this
will we know why it was this way.
Todo dolor cesa con muerte.
Sometimes even a stone will float
in the deep waters of the heart.

Lament for Mountains

Look, the night
is upon us.
The mountains have come

to darkness
and the last deer has given
itself to the hunter.

The trees are dissolving
into their own shadows.
The trumpet vine

has sounded its final call,
and the tap root
of the honeysuckle is pulling

its last breath of fragrance
from the earth.
The fox has no truck

with the rabbit
and the squirrel in its nest
dozes and twitches

while the bobcat
sharpens its perfect claws.
To have learned anything

in this life is to listen.
Still, no one hears
the blacksnake swallow

the robin's blue egg.
The cricket has ceased
its raspy saw

and there is no whisper
of water
from ephemeral streams,

nor any owl
or whippoorwill calling
in this dark.

Melding

Before the slow current of the Salt River
washes any memory of me away
I want to say
that the sun reflecting off the water
reminds me of the crystal chandelier
in the hallway of my grandmother's house
on the hill above the Braxton pond
where once, my mother watching
from the kitchen window, I sailed
my matchbox schooner in the cool of autumn,
where once with earthworm
and small, black cane pole
I caught my first bluegill,
where the cows of summer
stand belly-deep in the green water
and dragonflies perch
atop ironweeds' purple at the water's edge,
where the vee hint of watersnake
traverses the surface
and the dual beads of frog eyes
rise and sink in silence,
where brown turtle eggs
nestle high in the earthen dam
and the tadpoles churn
the water muddy in the hoofprints of cows,
where the muskrat
glides silently through the night
and the frogs bellow
late into the dark morning
while the stars dissolve in the gray mist.

What Drives Them

This morning the geese rise
honking in an easy storm of feathers.
They have spent the night in dream,
in the heavy dew of spring
grass, both bed and breakfast.

Now, as they lift themselves on air,
it is not the ferrite granules nesting
magnetically and incomprehensibly
in their frontal lobes, but something
else that leads them ever onward.

Somewhere beyond the trees, over
the next mountain, the grass is green,
the water pure and cloud-filled.
But now their life is sky and wing,
and all is that longing deep within.

Tonight they will settle once again
into an uneasy and ruffled slumber.
In the tall grass beside a farm pond
they will rest in fitful sleep, and dream
of endless horizons.

Searching

This is where we seldom venture at night
the hollow below the cemetery
where the fog lies heavy over the creek
where on a summer night
burrs cling to the wet legs of our jeans.

This is where we must go to find the cows
hulking silent and invisible in the dark
where first we hear them chewing
then we see our lantern light
gold in the brown of their eyes.

This is where the ironweed grows
taller than a man, where the bumblebees
nest in thick tangles of fescue.
Here we struggle
to tread lightly in the dark.

This is where the giant hackberry shades
the long-abandoned well
where the fingers of its roots
cling to the earth to stop its eroding
into the cavern beneath.

This is where we must take care
not to step into an unnoticed hole
where we place our ear to the ground
and listen to the mystery
of water deep and unseen.

Elegy for Me

When the black crow
comes for his corn
let me be standing knee-deep,
time forgotten in my pocket,
let a straw hat shade my eyes
and the sun dance on my face,
let the creel be full
of sunlight and rainbow,
let me know finally the secrets
of water, the twitch of rod,
the meaning
of each swirl and eddy,
let the reel sing
with no backlash,
my monofilament arching out forever.

CPSIA information can be obtained at www.ICGtesting.com
Printed in the USA
LVOW041313061011

249379LV00002BB/7/P